# THE BEST NBA
# TEAMS
## OF ALL TIME

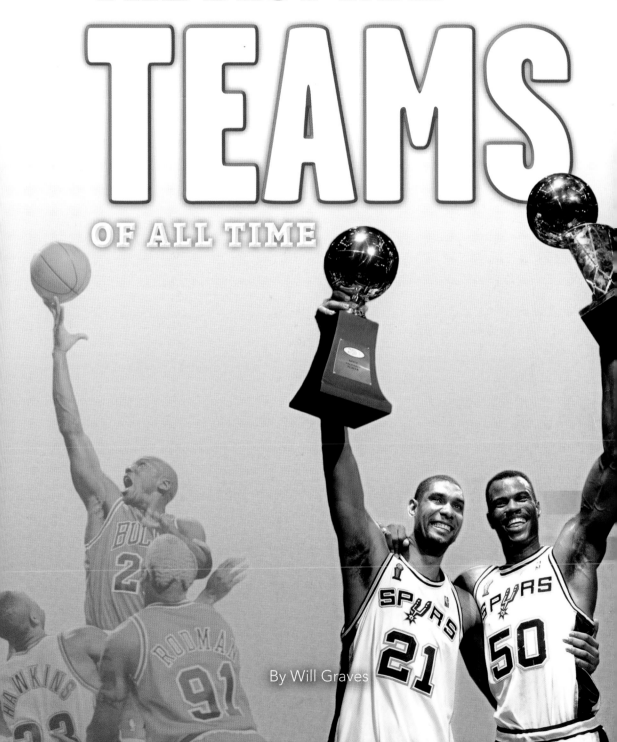

By Will Graves

www.abdopublishing.com

Published by Abdo Publishing, a division of ABDO, PO Box 398166, Minneapolis, Minnesota 55439. Copyright © 2015 by Abdo Consulting Group, Inc. International copyrights reserved in all countries. No part of this book may be reproduced in any form without written permission from the publisher. SportsZone™ is a trademark and logo of Abdo Publishing.

Printed in the United States of America, North Mankato, Minnesota
042014
092014

Cover Photos: Beth A. Keiser/AP Images (left);
Eric Gay/AP Images (right)
Interior Photos: Beth A. Keiser/AP Images, 1 (left), 4, 49; Eric Gay/AP Images, 1 (right), 5, 57; Matty Zimmerman/AP Images, 7; AP Images, 9, 11, 13, 15, 17, 19, 23, 25, 29; Dave Pickoff/AP Images, 21; Rusty Kennedy/AP Images, 27; Doug Pizac/AP Images, 31, 41; Steve Pyle/AP Images, 33; Mark Avery/AP Images, 35; Lennox Mclendon/AP Images, 37; Bob Galbraith/AP Images, 39; Fred Jewell/AP Images, 43; Charles Bennett/AP Images, 45, 47; Mark J. Terrill/AP Images, 51; Michael Caulfield/AP Images, 53; Kathy Willens/AP Images, 55; Wilfredo Lee/AP Images, 59; David Santiago/AP Images, 61

Editor: Chrös McDougall
Series Designer: Christa Schneider

**Library of Congress Control Number: 2014932899**

**Cataloging-in-Publication Data**
Graves, Will.
 The best NBA teams of all time / Will Graves.
  p. cm. -- (NBA's best ever)
ISBN 978-1-62403-414-5
1. National Basketball Association--Juvenile literature.     I. Title.
796.323--dc23

                                    2014932899

# TABLE OF CONTENTS

# INTRODUCTION

In the National Basketball Association (NBA), the ring is the thing.

Sure, fancy dunks and three-pointers are nice. But every team's goal is to win a championship and the special ring that comes along with it. Earning one ring is tough. Earning more than one is even tougher. That is why in the NBA, the best teams are the ones that reach the top and keep coming back for more. The greatest NBA teams in history have found different ways to win their rings. Some have played great defense. Others have scored a ton of points. And all of them have had one thing in common. They wanted the ring more than anyone else.

# Here are some of the best teams in NBA history.

# 1952-53
# MINNEAPOLIS
# LAKERS

**George Mikan was the NBA's first true giant.** The Minneapolis Lakers' 6-foot-10 center stood tall over the new league. So did his team.

The Lakers began playing in 1947. That was a time when basketball was not nearly as popular as it is today. The NBA had only begun in 1946. It didn't take the NBA name until 1949–50. That was one year after the Lakers joined. Before then, the team played one season in the National Basketball League. But it did not matter in which league the Lakers played. They played well anywhere. The Lakers won six championships between 1948 and 1954. The 1952–53 team might have been their best.

Mikan was in the prime of his career that season. He was becoming famous, too. Fans of other teams made sure to get tickets to see him play when the Lakers were in town.

Minneapolis Lakers forward Vern Mikkelsen puts up a shot during a 1953 game against the New York Knicks.

**The Lakers were not just a one-man show, though.** Teams tried to focus on Mikan. But he would just pass to speedy guard Slater Martin. If Martin was covered, Mikan would flip the ball to forward Vern Mikkelsen. If that failed, veteran forward Jim Pollard was ready to go.

Coach John Kundla's job was to make sure each of his players was sharp. The Lakers went 48–22 during the regular season. And they saved their best basketball for the playoffs. The Fort Wayne Pistons nearly upset the Lakers in the Western Division finals. But Minneapolis won in the deciding fifth game. That sent the team to the NBA Finals. There, they beat the New York Knicks four games to one.

Minneapolis again won the championship in 1954. But the team went downhill after that. Mikan retired, and the Lakers started to lose. In 1960, new owners moved the team to Los Angeles.

# .390

**The Lakers' shooting percentage in 1952–53. It was the second-highest total in the league.**

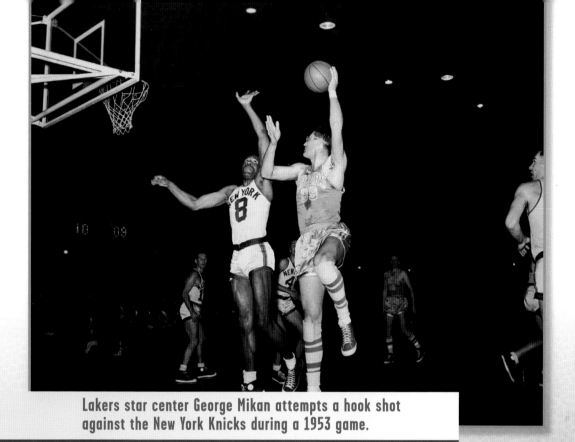

Lakers star center George Mikan attempts a hook shot against the New York Knicks during a 1953 game.

# 1952–53 MINNEAPOLIS LAKERS

### KEY STATS AND PLAYERS

**Record:** 48–22

**Postseason:** Defeated the New York Knicks 4–1 in the NBA Finals

**Slater Martin**

**Position:** Guard

**Age:** 27

**Key Stat:** .780 free-throw percentage

**George Mikan**

**Position:** Center

**Age:** 28

**Key Stat:** 14.4 rebounds per game, a league best

**Vern Mikkelsen**

**Position:** Forward

**Age:** 24

**Key Stat:** 9.3 rebounds per game

**Jim Pollard**

**Position:** Forward

**Age:** 30

**Key Stat:** 13.0 points per game

# 1962–63
# BOSTON
# CELTICS

**Arnold "Red" Auerbach loved to win.**
And when his Boston Celtics won, the coach was known for lighting a victory cigar. The ritual drove other teams crazy. So Auerbach promised to stop if one of them could beat his Celtics.

Few teams did during the 1960s. Boston won 10 championships between 1959 and 1969. The Celtics were at their very best in 1962–63. Boston had it all that season. Nine of the team's 13 players and Auerbach would one day make it to the Hall of Fame.

Point guard Bob Cousy was in his final season. He kept the offense humming and averaged 6.8 assists per game. Center Bill Russell was in his prime. He averaged 16.8 points and 23.6 rebounds per game. He also was the league's best defensive player. That helped him win the NBA's Most Valuable Player (MVP) Award.

Boston Celtics center Bill Russell flies to the basket during a 1963 game against the Syracuse Nationals.

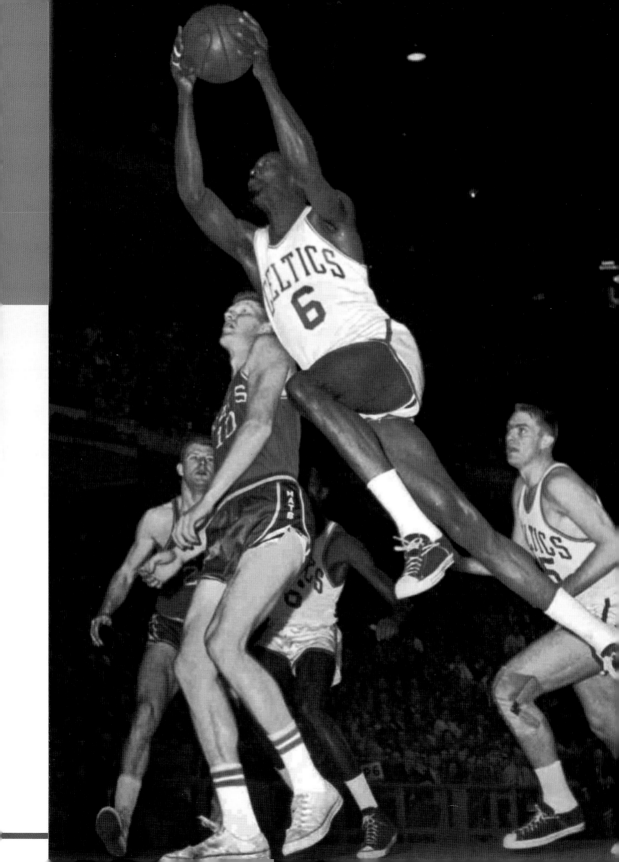

**Guard Sam Jones led the team in scoring with 19.7 points per game.** Rookie forward John Havlicek did a little bit of everything. Guard Tom Heinsohn made 84 percent of his free throws. And K. C. Jones was a key reserve. He would later coach the Celtics to two NBA titles in the 1980s.

**1,960**

**Boston's league-leading assist total in 1962–63.**

The Celtics won a league-best 58 games in 1962–63. They had trouble in the playoffs, though. The conference finals went to Game 7. But Sam Jones scored 47 points in the deciding game. That helped the Celtics pull away in the second half for a 142–131 victory over the Cincinnati Royals.

Things went a little smoother in the Finals. Boston beat the Los Angeles Lakers in six games. The season ended with Auerbach lighting one last cigar to celebrate a job well done.

Celtics coach Red Auerbach, *left*, huddles with his veterans before a 1963 playoff game against the Cincinnati Royals.

# 1962–63 BOSTON CELTICS

## KEY STATS AND PLAYERS

**Record:** 58–22

**Postseason:** Defeated the Los Angeles Lakers 4–2 to win the NBA title

| | |
|---|---|
| **John Havlicek** | **Sam Jones** |
| **Position:** Forward | **Position:** Guard |
| **Age:** 22 | **Age:** 29 |
| **Key Stat:** 14.3 points per game | **Key Stat:** 19.7 points per game |
| **Tom Heinsohn** | **Bill Russell** |
| **Position:** Forward | **Position:** Center |
| **Age:** 28 | **Age:** 28 |
| **Key Stat:** .835 free-throw percentage | **Key Stat:** 23.6 rebounds per game |

# 1966–67 PHILADELPHIA 76ERS

**Wilt Chamberlain made playing basketball look easy.** Of course, for "Wilt the Stilt," it was. He was 7 feet 1 inch tall and 275 pounds. That made him a giant among giants. He had entered the league in 1959. And he was immediately the NBA's biggest star. He could score points like no other player. Few could match his rebounding, either.

All those points and rebounds had not led to a title, though. Finally, in 1966–67, Chamberlain had his breakthrough. Having help from some future Hall of Fame players helped, too.

The Philadelphia 76ers' Wilt Chamberlain, *right*, battles with Boston Celtics center Bill Russell for a rebound in 1967.

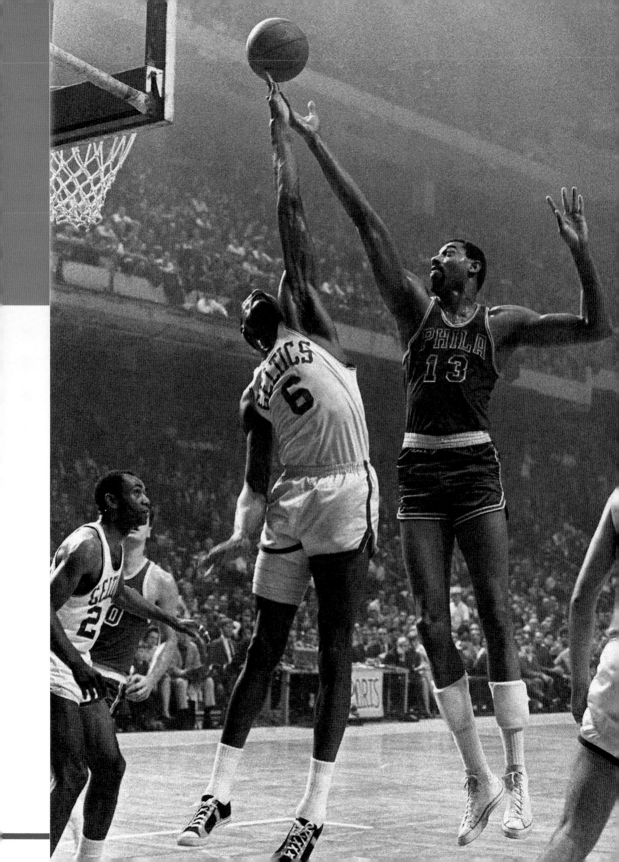

**Chamberlain's Philadelphia 76ers won 68 games that season.** That was a record at the time. Chamberlain was almost impossible to guard one-on-one. Teams would have to use two or three players to slow him down. But the double teams would leave one of Chamberlain's teammates open. And he had more than one teammate who knew what to do with the ball in his hands. There was sharp-shooting guard Hal Greer. There was brawny forward Chet Walker. And there was young Billy Cunningham. He was one of the best defenders of his generation.

The 76ers did not cruise through the season. They steamrolled their way to the top like a team on a mission. They won 26 of their first 28 games. And no one could catch them after that. The playoffs were more of the same. Philadelphia went 7–2 in the first two rounds of the playoffs. Then it dispatched the San Francisco Warriors in six games in the NBA Finals.

# 125.2

**The number of points per game the 76ers averaged. It was the highest in the league.**

The 76ers celebrate in the locker room after beating the Boston Celtics in the 1967 playoffs.

# 1966–67 PHILADELPHIA 76ERS

## KEY STATS AND PLAYERS

**Record:** 68–13

**Postseason:** Defeated the San Francisco Warriors 4–2 in the NBA Finals

### Wilt Chamberlain
**Position:** Center
**Age:** 30
**Key Stat:** 24.2 rebounds per game

### Hal Greer
**Position:** Guard
**Age:** 30
**Key Stat:** 22.1 points per game

### Billy Cunningham
**Position:** Forward
**Age:** 23
**Key Stat:** 7.3 rebounds per game

### Chet Walker
**Position:** Forward
**Age:** 26
**Key Stat:** 23.3 points per game in the NBA Finals

# 1969–70
# NEW YORK KNICKS

**Willis Reed could barely walk, let alone play basketball.** It was the 1970 NBA Finals. The New York Knicks' center had torn a muscle in his right thigh during Game 5. The injury kept the league's MVP out of Game 6. And without him, the Knicks were no match for the Los Angeles Lakers. So it all came down to the deciding Game 7.

No one was sure if Reed would play. But then he limped onto the floor at Madison Square Garden. The home crowd erupted. The Lakers were stunned. They stopped their own warm-ups to watch him.

"I didn't want to have to look at myself in the mirror 20 years later and say I wished I had tried to play," Reed said.

New York Knicks center Willis Reed, *right*, goes up for a shot against the Los Angeles Lakers during the 1970 NBA Finals.

**That is when the Knicks knew the Lakers did not have a chance.** Reed scored New York's first two baskets. Guard Walt "Clyde" Frazier did the rest. He scored 36 points and had 19 assists. The Knicks won 113–99 to claim their first NBA title.

# 105.9

The Knicks' opponents' scoring average in 1969–70. It was the lowest in the NBA.

The Knicks had spent all season proving they were the best team in the league. They played the kind of in-your-face defense other teams could not handle. That helped them start the year 23–1.

Frazier was the engine that drove New York. He was known for his flashy clothes off the court and his quick hands on it. Frazier would hound opponents all over the floor. His play complimented Reed's, who was a force under the basket. It was a combination few teams could solve.

Knicks guard Walt Frazier keeps the ball away from a Los Angeles Lakers defender during the 1970 NBA Finals.

# 1969–70 NEW YORK KNICKS
## KEY STATS AND PLAYERS

**Record:** 60–22

**Postseason:** Defeated the Los Angeles Lakers 4–3 in the NBA Finals

### Bill Bradley
**Position:** Forward
**Age:** 26
**Key Stat:** .824 free-throw percentage

### Dave DeBusschere
**Position:** Forward
**Age:** 29
**Key Stat:** 10.0 rebounds per game

### Walt Frazier
**Position:** Guard
**Age:** 24
**Key Stat:** 8.2 assists per game

### Willis Reed
**Position:** Center
**Age:** 27
**Key Stat:** 21.7 points per game

# 1971–72
# LOS ANGELES LAKERS

**If you were building the greatest team ever, what would you need?** A dominant center? OK. A sharp-shooting guard? Great. How about two of them? Even better.

The Los Angeles Lakers had all three in 1971–72. Even at age 35, center Wilt Chamberlain was still one of the best big men in the league. Guard Jerry West was in his prime as one of the best guards in NBA history. And Gail Goodrich was every bit as good of a shooter as West. Both Goodrich and West averaged more than 25 points per game that season.

Los Angeles Lakers center Wilt Chamberlain leaps to shoot over two Boston Celtics defenders during a 1972 game.

**For two glorious months, the Lakers were the best team to ever lace up high tops.** On November 5, 1971, they began a winning streak that ran through January 7, 1972. The team took the floor 33 times during that stretch. The Lakers left the floor as winners each time. It is a record no team has come close to breaking through 2013. And the games were not even close. Only twice did an opponent come within five points of the Lakers. Eight times the Lakers won by at least 20 points. Once they won by 44!

The streak finally ended on January 9, 1972. The Lakers lost on the road to the Milwaukee Bucks. It turned out to be just a speed bump.

# 121.0

**The Lakers' league-leading scoring average in 1971–72. That was nearly five points more than the next team.**

The Lakers won 69 games that season. That was a record at the time. They were even better in the playoffs. Los Angeles roared to the NBA Finals and beat the New York Knicks in five games.

Lakers guard Jerry West dribbles around a Houston Rockets defender during a December 1971 game.

# 1971–72 LOS ANGELES LAKERS

### KEY STATS AND PLAYERS

**Record:** 69–13

**Postseason:** Defeated the New York Knicks 4–1 in the NBA Finals

**Wilt Chamberlain**

**Position:** Center

**Age:** 35

**Key Stat:** 19.2 rebounds per game, a league best

**Happy Hairston**

**Position:** Forward

**Age:** 29

**Key Stat:** 13.1 points and rebounds per game

**Gail Goodrich**

**Position:** Guard

**Age:** 28

**Key Stat:** 25.9 points per game

**Jerry West**

**Position:** Guard

**Age:** 33

**Key Stat:** 9.7 assists per game, a league best

25

# 1982–83 PHILADELPHIA 76ERS

**Moses Malone was a giant of a man.**
At times he even talked like a giant. The Philadelphia 76ers' center was asked how his team would do in the 1983 playoffs. He replied simply, "fo', fo', fo'." It was his way of saying the Sixers would sweep all three rounds of the postseason in four games each.

As it turned out, Malone's prediction was off. But only by a little bit. Philadelphia lost one game during the playoffs. It hardly mattered, though. The team otherwise cruised to its first championship in 16 years.

What made the 76ers different that year was Malone. Philadelphia had been good for years thanks to star Julius Erving. The man nicknamed "Dr. J" was one of the greatest players of all time. And he helped make the slam dunk popular. Still, Erving needed some help if the Sixers were to become champions.

Philadelphia 76ers center Moses Malone goes up for a shot against the Milwaukee Bucks during the 1983 playoffs.

**Erving got that help when the Sixers traded for Malone before the 1982–83 season.** Opposing teams had to focus on Malone. That left Erving and guards Andrew Toney and Maurice Cheeks with plenty of room to work. Cheeks was like the team's quarterback. He was always making sure his teammates were where they needed to be. Toney was the tough-as-nails defender.

Malone, though, stood above them all. He had the size of a center at 6 feet 10 inches. But he had the quickness of a forward. Even the great Los Angeles Lakers center Kareem Abdul-Jabbar could not keep up with Malone in the NBA Finals. Philadelphia romped to a title in a "fo'"-game sweep.

# 12–1

**Philadelphia's record in the 1982–83 playoffs. It was the second-best postseason record in NBA history through 2013.**

The 76ers' Julius Erving, *left*, and Moses Malone hold the NBA championship trophy in 1983.

# 1982–83 PHILADELPHIA 76ERS
### KEY STATS AND PLAYERS

**Record:** 65–17

**Postseason:** Defeated the Los Angeles Lakers 4–0 in the NBA Finals

### Maurice Cheeks
**Position:** Guard
**Age:** 26
**Key Stat:** 2.3 steals per game

### Julius Erving
**Position:** Forward
**Age:** 32
**Key Stat:** 21.4 points per game

### Moses Malone
**Position:** Center
**Age:** 27
**Key Stat:** 15.3 rebounds per game, a league best

### Andrew Toney
**Position:** Guard
**Age:** 25
**Key Stat:** 19.7 points per game

# 1983-84 BOSTON CELTICS

**Larry Bird spent five years hoping to get a second chance at Earvin "Magic" Johnson.** The two first faced off in the 1979 college championship game. It was not exactly a fair fight. Johnson's Michigan State University team was loaded. Indiana State University had Bird as its only star. And indeed, Michigan State won.

But things were different in the NBA. Bird's Boston Celtics met Johnson's Los Angeles Lakers three times in the NBA Finals. The first meeting was in 1984. Bird's Celtics had size in center Robert Parish and forward Kevin McHale. They had shooting from guard Danny Ainge. They had defense from guard Dennis Johnson. They had playmaking from forward Cedric Maxwell. And they had Bird. "Larry Legend" was one of the NBA's best all-around players.

Boston Celtics forward Larry Bird shoots over the Los Angeles Lakers' Kareem Abdul-Jabbar during the 1984 NBA Finals.

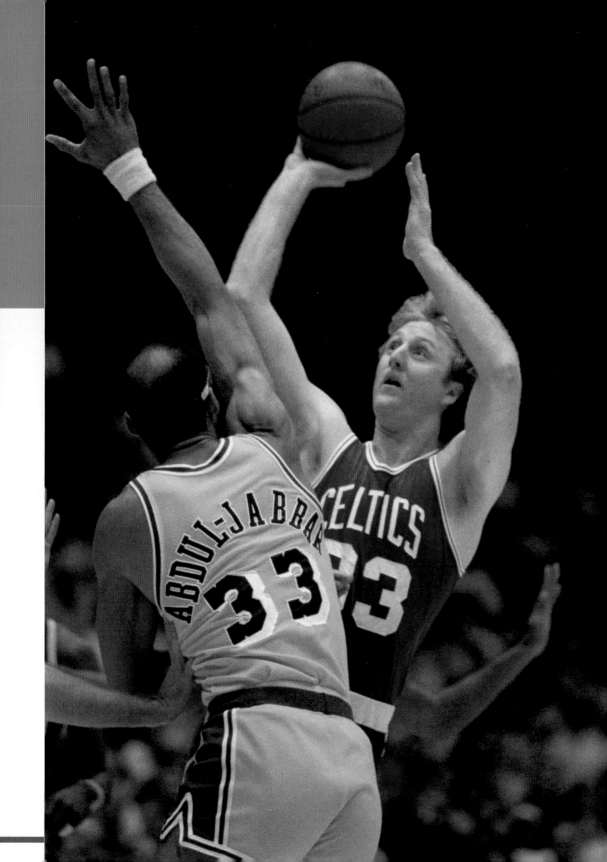

**Bird averaged 24.2 points, 10.1 rebounds, 6.6 assists, and 1.8 steals per game that year.** It was little surprise when he was named the NBA's MVP.

Boston had no trouble in the regular season. The Celtics won the Atlantic Division by a whopping 10 games. Then they survived a fierce test in the playoffs to reach the NBA Finals. There, Johnson and his Lakers awaited.

The rival teams went back and forth for six games. The Celtics had a chance to clinch in Game 6. But the Lakers pulled away late for a 119–108 win.

Bird finally got his revenge in Game 7. He also got some help. Maxwell took over the show. He scored 24 points. Plus he added eight rebounds and eight assists. The Celtics won 111–102. Bird had finally proven that he was Johnson's equal. But their rivalry was just heating up.

# 33–8

Boston's home record during the 1983–84 regular season.

Celtics forward Kevin McHale drives to the basket during a 1984 playoff game against the Milwaukee Bucks.

# 1983–84 BOSTON CELTICS

## KEY STATS AND PLAYERS

**Record:** 62–20

**Postseason:** Defeated the Los Angeles Lakers 4–3 in the NBA Finals

### Larry Bird

**Position:** Forward

**Age:** 27

**Key Stat:** .888 free-throw percentage, a league best

### Kevin McHale

**Position:** Forward

**Age:** 26

**Key Stat:** .556 field goal percentage

### Dennis Johnson

**Position:** Guard

**Age:** 29

**Key Stat:** 16.6 points per game in the playoffs

### Robert Parish

**Position:** Center

**Age:** 30

**Key Stat:** 3.0 offensive rebounds per game

# 1986–87
# LOS ANGELES LAKERS

**The Los Angeles Lakers had long been Kareem Abdul-Jabbar's team.** And for good reason. The center was one of the greatest players in league history. Through 2013, he was still the league's all-time leading scorer. Many of his points came on his unstoppable skyhook shot.

But Abdul-Jabbar turned 40 before the 1987 playoffs. He was one of the oldest players in the league. So it was time for Earvin "Magic" Johnson to take over.

Johnson already was the NBA's best passer. Now coach Pat Riley wanted Johnson to start scoring more. It was a role Johnson embraced. He averaged a career-high 23.9 points in 1986–87. And he still led the NBA with 12.2 assists per game. The Lakers went 65–17 that season with Johnson running the "Showtime" fast breaks. But Johnson hardly did it alone.

Los Angeles Lakers guard Earvin "Magic" Johnson defends against the Seattle SuperSonics during the 1987 playoffs.

**Forward James Worthy was an All-Star.** He was one of the most athletic players around. Guard Byron Scott could shoot the lights out. And guard Michael Cooper and his long arms hounded opponents. That helped make him the NBA's Defensive Player of the Year.

# 15-3

**The Los Angeles Lakers' record in the 1987 postseason.**

The Lakers stormed to the NBA Finals. There they met the Boston Celtics for the third time in four years. Los Angeles easily won the first two games. Then the Celtics won Game 3. Boston was leading by a point in the final seconds of Game 4, too. That is when Johnson worked his magic. The clock was winding down. Johnson dribbled to the middle of the lane. Then he offered up his own version of Abdul-Jabbar's famous skyhook.

The ball splashed through the net. The Lakers went on their way to beating the Celtics in six games. The torch had been passed.

The Lakers' Magic Johnson, *left*, and coach Pat Riley celebrate after winning the 1987 NBA title.

# 1986–87 LOS ANGELES LAKERS

## KEY STATS AND PLAYERS

**Record:** 65–17

**Postseason:** Defeated the Boston Celtics 4–2 in the NBA Finals

### Kareem Abdul-Jabbar

**Position:** Center

**Age:** 39

**Key Stat:** .564 field-goal percentage

### Earvin "Magic" Johnson

**Position:** Guard

**Age:** 27

**Key Stat:** 26.2 points per game in the NBA Finals

### Byron Scott

**Position:** Guard

**Age:** 25

**Key Stat:** .436 three-point shooting percentage

### James Worthy

**Position:** Forward

**Age:** 25

**Key Stat:** 19.4 points per game

# 1988–89 DETROIT PISTONS

**The Detroit Pistons fell to the Los Angeles Lakers in Game 7 of the 1988 NBA Finals.** They took out their pain on the rest of the league in 1988–89.

The NBA at the time was known for the dazzling play of Earvin "Magic" Johnson, Larry Bird, and Michael Jordan. But Detroit offered something different. The Pistons were called the "Bad Boys." They played a rough-and-tumble style that angered opponents. Detroit did not really care about that, though. All the Pistons wanted to do was win.

Guards Isiah Thomas and Joe Dumars took care of the offense. Thomas averaged 18.2 points per game while Dumars scored 17.2. Center Bill Laimbeer and forwards Rick Mahorn and Dennis Rodman took care of the defense. They combined for 25.9 rebounds per game—and more than their share of fouls.

Detroit Pistons forward Dennis Rodman puts up a reverse layup against the Los Angeles Lakers in the 1989 NBA Finals.

**The Pistons even found a way to stop Jordan and his Chicago Bulls.**
Detroit coach Chuck Daly came up with a plan called "The Jordan Rules." Following them, the Pistons were able to keep Jordan under wraps whenever the two teams met.

Detroit had similar success against the Lakers in the NBA Finals. Los Angeles had won the previous two NBA titles. But the team was hurting this time.

The Lakers lost guard Byron Scott to injury before Game 1 and Johnson to injury in Game 2. They did not stand a chance after that. The Pistons won the first four games of the series to take their first championship in a sweep. Then they won another one in 1990. As it turned out, the "Bad Boys" were pretty good after all.

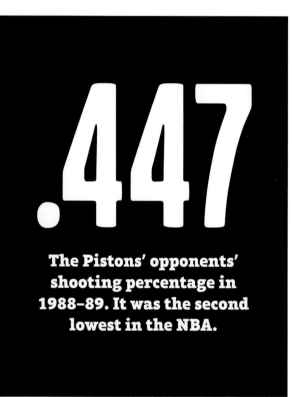

**.447**

**The Pistons' opponents' shooting percentage in 1988–89. It was the second lowest in the NBA.**

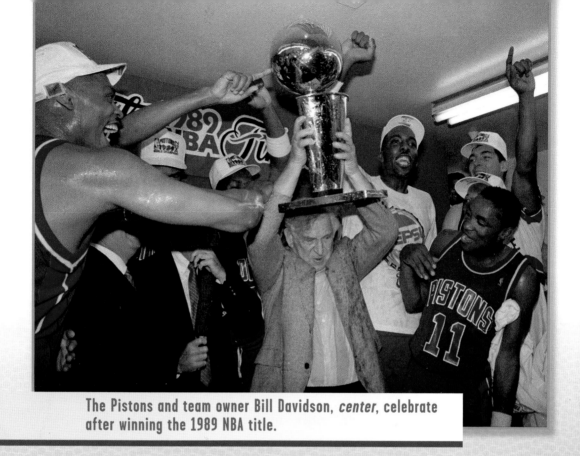

The Pistons and team owner Bill Davidson, *center*, celebrate after winning the 1989 NBA title.

# 1988–89 DETROIT PISTONS

### KEY STATS AND PLAYERS

**Record:** 63–19

**Postseason:** Defeated the Los Angeles Lakers 4–0 in the NBA Finals

**Joe Dumars**

**Position:** Guard

**Age:** 25

**Key Stat:** 27.3 points per game in the NBA Finals

**Vinnie Johnson**

**Position:** Guard

**Age:** 32

**Key Stat:** 13.8 points per game off the bench

**Bill Laimbeer**

**Position:** Center

**Age:** 31

**Key Stat:** 9.6 rebounds per game

**Isiah Thomas**

**Position:** Guard

**Age:** 27

**Key Stat:** 8.3 assists per game

# 1991-92
# CHICAGO BULLS

**Michael Jordan pulled up at the three-point line and let the ball fly.** The Chicago Bulls' star was known more for his soaring dunks than for his shooting range. But for that one night, it did not matter. The ball sailed through the air and swished through the net. It was Jordan's sixth three-pointer of the first half in Game 1 of the 1992 NBA Finals.

Jordan threw his hands up and shrugged his shoulders. Even Jordan could not believe his long-range success. The rest of the NBA could not believe it either.

Jordan was at the peak of his Hall of Fame career in 1991–92. He had been the game's best player for a few years. Now he had the game's best team to play with him.

Chicago Bulls guard Michael Jordan shoots over a Portland Trail Blazers defender during Game 1 of the 1992 NBA Finals.

**Jordan averaged 30.1 points per game that season while winning the league's MVP Award.** He had the perfect sidekick in forward Scottie Pippen. Pippen would have been the top player on just about any other team in the league. But that did not bother Pippen. He averaged 21.0 points, 7.7 rebounds, and 7.0 assists per game for the Bulls in 1991–92.

The Bulls had won the title in 1991. But they might have been even better in 1992. Chicago went 67–15 that year to easily win the Central Division. The New York Knicks posed a tough challenge in the second round of the playoffs. But the Bulls beat them in seven games. By the time they reached the NBA Finals, they were running on all cylinders. Chicago beat the Portland Trail Blazers in six games to win a second straight championship.

# .508

The Bulls' team field-goal percentage in 1991–92. That led the NBA.

The Bulls' Michael Jordan, *left*, and Scottie Pippen slap hands as the team celebrates in Game 1 of the 1992 NBA Finals.

# 1991–92 CHICAGO BULLS

## KEY STATS AND PLAYERS

**Record:** 67–15

**Postseason:** Defeated the Portland Trail Blazers 4–2 in the NBA Finals

### B. J. Armstrong

**Position:** Guard

**Age:** 24

**Key Stat:** .402 three-point shooting percentage

### Michael Jordan

**Position:** Guard

**Age:** 28

**Key Stat:** 35.8 points per game in the NBA Finals

### Horace Grant

**Position:** Forward

**Age:** 26

**Key Stat:** 1.6 blocks per game

### Scottie Pippen

**Position:** Forward

**Age:** 26

**Key Stat:** 7.7 rebounds per game

# 1995-96
# CHICAGO BULLS

**The buzzer sounded to give the Chicago Bulls their fourth NBA title.**

Bulls guard Michael Jordan grabbed the ball and would not let go. He then ran off the floor and found a small room where he laid on the ground and cried.

The superstar guard had taken a season and a half off from basketball, returning in March 1995. And he had wondered if he would ever again be a champion. He and the Bulls answered that question and then some in 1995–96.

Over nine months, Chicago put together the best season in NBA history. The Bulls won a record 72 games. And they did it with a slightly different style than the one they had used to win three championships in a row from 1991 to 1993.

The Chicago Bulls' Randy Brown hugs teammate Michael Jordan after the team won the 1996 NBA title.

**Jordan was a little older now.** At age 32, he did not fly quite as high as he used to. It was not exactly a problem, though. Jordan was still an explosive force. He improved his jump shot. Plus he remained one of the league's top defenders.

Scottie Pippen was again right by Jordan's side. They were still the best one-two punch in the league. And in 1995, Dennis Rodman joined them. Rodman was famous for his wacky hairstyles. Sometimes his hair would be white. Sometimes it would be purple. No matter what color it was, though, Rodman could rebound. He was one of the best rebounders of all time.

**105.2**

**Chicago's league-leading scoring average in 1995–96.**

Chicago tore through the playoffs. The Bulls lost just three times in the postseason. They beat the Seattle SuperSonics in six games in the NBA Finals. As Jordan ran off the floor for a private moment, the league had its proof. Michael Jordan was back.

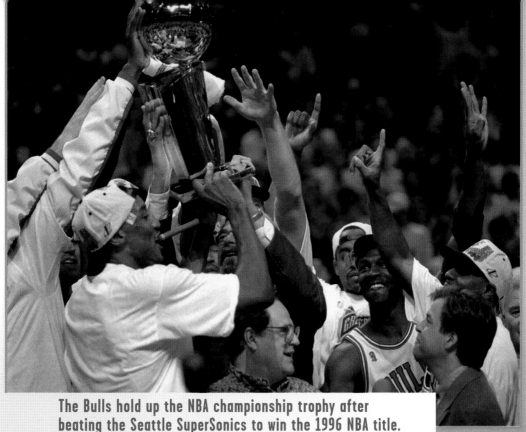

The Bulls hold up the NBA championship trophy after beating the Seattle SuperSonics to win the 1996 NBA title.

# 1995–96 CHICAGO BULLS

## KEY STATS AND PLAYERS

**Record:** 72–10

**Postseason:** Defeated the Seattle SuperSonics 4–2 in the NBA Finals

### Michael Jordan

**Position:** Guard

**Age:** 32

**Key Stat:** 30.4 points per game, a league best

### Toni Kukoc

**Position:** Forward

**Age:** 27

**Key Stat:** .490 field-goal percentage

### Scottie Pippen

**Position:** Forward

**Age:** 30

**Key Stat:** 19.4 points per game

### Dennis Rodman

**Position:** Forward

**Age:** 34

**Key Stat:** 14.9 rebounds per game, a league best

# 1999–2000
# LOS ANGELES LAKERS

**Shaquille O'Neal and Kobe Bryant were great individual players.** But they needed to learn to play together. Coach Phil Jackson had helped Michael Jordan and Scottie Pippen become great teammates. Together the trio had won six NBA titles with the Chicago Bulls. In 1999, the Los Angeles Lakers hired Jackson to recreate the magic.

Getting O'Neal and Bryant on the same page proved difficult. Both players were outstanding scorers. And each loved to have the ball in his hands. But there was just one ball to go around. Jackson gave both players books to read. The books talked about things such as being humble and taking pride in being a champion. They worked. At 67–15, the Lakers posted the NBA's best record that season.

Los Angeles Lakers guard Kobe Bryant drives to the basket against the Portland Trail Blazers during the 2000 playoffs.

**O'Neal had perhaps the finest season of his career.** He averaged 29.7 points, 13.6 rebounds, and 3.8 assists per game. He easily won the MVP Award. Bryant, playing in his fourth season, grew up on the job. He averaged 22.5 points per game. He also was named to the NBA's All-Defensive Team.

The key moment of the season for O'Neal and Bryant came in the playoffs. It was Game 7 of the Western Conference finals. The Lakers trailed the Portland Trail Blazers by 15 points in the second half. Then Los Angeles started its comeback. The Lakers rallied to win. One of the key baskets came on an alley-oop from Bryant to O'Neal. The burly center pointed at Bryant after the play as if to say "thank you."

The two had finally learned how to share. And after the Lakers beat the Indiana Pacers in the NBA Finals, they went on to win NBA titles in 2001 and 2002, as well.

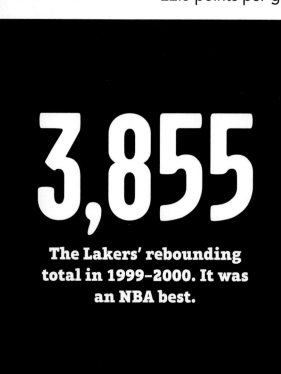

# 3,855

**The Lakers' rebounding total in 1999–2000. It was an NBA best.**

Lakers center Shaquille O'Neal holds the NBA championship trophy, *left*, and his NBA Finals MVP trophy in 2000.

# 1999–2000 LOS ANGELES LAKERS

## KEY STATS AND PLAYERS

**Record:** 67–15

**Postseason:** Defeated the Indiana Pacers 4–2 in the NBA Finals

**Kobe Bryant**

**Position:** Guard

**Age:** 21

**Key Stat:** 4.9 assists per game

**Ron Harper**

**Position:** Guard

**Age:** 36

**Key Stat:** 3.4 assists per game

**Shaquille O'Neal**

**Position:** Center

**Age:** 27

**Key Stat:** 38.0 points per game in the NBA Finals

**Glen Rice**

**Position:** Forward

**Age:** 32

**Key Stat:** .418 three-point shooting percentage in the playoffs

# 2002–03
# SAN ANTONIO SPURS

**The 2002–03 season marked a changing of the guard for the San Antonio Spurs.** Center David "The Admiral" Robinson had long been the team's star player. Forward Tim Duncan was a star on the rise. In Robinson's final season, Duncan officially took over.

Together the "Twin Towers" had already led the Spurs to the 1999 NBA title. But the 1999 season had been quirky. A labor dispute meant the regular season was shortened to just 50 games. So in 2002–03, the Spurs proved they could win during a full season as well.

San Antonio won 60 of its 82 games in 2002–03. That tied the Spurs for the NBA's best record. Meanwhile, Duncan earned his second MVP Award. He averaged 23.3 points, 12.9 rebounds, and 3.9 assists per game.

San Antonio Spurs forward Tim Duncan blocks New Jersey Nets center Dikembe Mutombo's shot during the 2003 NBA Finals.

**Duncan was not flashy like some other players.** He just did everything well. He could shoot jumpers. He could dunk the ball. He could block shots. He could rebound. And he could pass.

The Spurs built a team around Duncan. Second-year point guard Tony Parker had a breakout season. Malik Rose was not the biggest forward in the NBA at just 6 feet 7 inches. But his hustle made it tough for larger players to keep up with him.

The Spurs did not crush other teams. They just found a way to win. San Antonio won each of its four playoff series in six games. In the NBA Finals, the New Jersey Nets tied the series at two games each. Then the Spurs clamped down on defense. New Jersey did not break 83 points in Game 5 or Game 6. The Spurs and their Twin Towers were again champions.

# 529

**The number of shots the Spurs blocked in 2002–03. It was an NBA best.**

Tim Duncan, *left*, and David Robinson, *right*, celebrate the Spurs' 2003 title with NBA commissioner David Stern.

# 2002–03 SAN ANTONIO SPURS

### KEY STATS AND PLAYERS

**Record:** 60–22

**Postseason:** Defeated the New Jersey Nets 4–2 in the NBA Finals

---

### Tim Duncan

**Position:** Forward

**Age:** 26

**Key Stat:** 17.0 rebounds per game in the NBA Finals

---

### Manu Ginobili

**Position:** Guard

**Age:** 25

**Key Stat:** 1.4 steals per game

### Tony Parker

**Position:** Guard

**Age:** 20

**Key Stat:** 5.3 assists per game

---

### David Robinson

**Position:** Center

**Age:** 37

**Key Stat:** 7.9 rebounds per game

# 2012-13
# MIAMI HEAT

**LeBron James always goes big.** Before the 2010–11 season, James and center Chris Bosh signed with the Miami Heat. The team already had superstar guard Dwyane Wade. Expectations were high. Before the season, James told fans he wanted to win "not one, not two," but as many championships as he could. By the end of the 2012–13 season, the "Big Three" were on their way.

The Heat won it all in 2012. That took a lot of pressure off the players. Their first title in hand, James and his teammates focused on becoming a dynasty. The 2012–13 Heat team was even better than it had been the year before. Miami won 66 games in all. That included 27 straight between February 3 and March 25.

Miami Heat forward LeBron James posts up against the San Antonio Spurs' Boris Diaw in Game 7 of the 2013 NBA Finals.

**James won his fourth MVP Award that year.** During the season, he averaged 26.8 points, 8.0 rebounds, and 7.3 assists per game. Wade shook off injuries to average 21.2 points per game. And Bosh played the steady third wheel to the two superstars.

The Heat made the regular season look easy. The playoffs were harder. Miami needed seven games to escape the upset-minded Indiana Pacers in the Eastern Conference finals. Then the San Antonio Spurs stood in the Heat's way of a second straight championship. And the Spurs almost did it.

San Antonio took a five-point lead with 28 seconds left in the fourth quarter of Game 6. Miami fans started heading for the exits, thinking the series was over. But they were wrong. Miami guard Ray Allen hit a three-pointer to tie it. The Heat won in overtime and then won Game 7. Miami had secured back-to-back titles—just like James knew the Heat would.

## .536

Miami's field goal percentage on two-point shots in 2012–13. It was the best in the league.

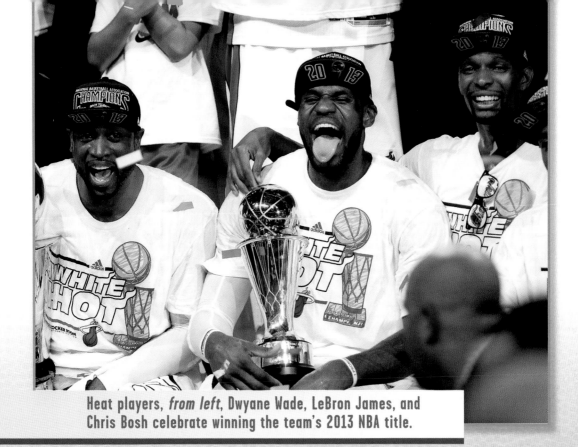

Heat players, *from left*, Dwyane Wade, LeBron James, and Chris Bosh celebrate winning the team's 2013 NBA title.

# 2012–13 MIAMI HEAT

## KEY STATS AND PLAYERS

**Record:** 66–16

**Postseason:** Defeated the San Antonio Spurs 4-3 to win the NBA title

**Ray Allen**
Position: Guard
Age: 37
Key Stat: 139 three-point baskets

**Chris Bosh**
Position: Center
Age: 28
Key Stat: 1.4 blocks per game

**LeBron James**
Position: Forward
Age: 28
Key Stat: 10.9 rebounds per game in the NBA Finals

**Dwyane Wade**
Position: Guard
Age: 31
Key Stat: 21.2 points per game

# HONORABLE MENTIONS

**1957–58 St. Louis Hawks** – Forward Bob Pettit helped the Hawks upset the favored Boston Celtics 4–2 in the NBA Finals.

**1970–71 Milwaukee Bucks** – Center Lew Alcindor (later known as Kareem Abdul-Jabbar) and point guard Oscar Robertson led the Bucks to a 66–16 record and a sweep of the Baltimore Bullets in the NBA Finals.

**1976–77 Portland Trail Blazers** – Center Bill Walton and forward Maurice Lucas pushed the Blazers to the title by storming through the postseason with a 14–5 record.

**1979–80 Los Angeles Lakers** – Rookie guard Earvin "Magic" Johnson did it all, including playing center in Game 6 of the NBA Finals as the Lakers beat the Philadelphia 76ers for the title.

**1994–95 Houston Rockets** – Center Hakeem "The Dream" Olajuwon took advantage of Michael Jordan's retirement as the Rockets won their second NBA title in a row, crushing the Orlando Magic 4–0 in the NBA Finals.

**1998–99 San Antonio Spurs** – Led by forward Tim Duncan, the Spurs went 37–13 in the lockout-shortened season, and then beat the New York Knicks 4–1 in the NBA Finals.

**2003–04 Detroit Pistons** – Bad Boys 2? Point guard Chauncey Billups guided the defensive-minded Pistons to a 4–3 upset over the Lakers in the NBA Finals.

**2007–08 Boston Celtics** – Forwards Kevin Garnett and Paul Pierce and guard Ray Allen formed a three-headed monster as the Celtics edged the Lakers 4–2 in the NBA Finals. It was Boston's first title since 1986.

**2008–09 Los Angeles Lakers** – Guard Kobe Bryant proved he could win without center Shaquille O'Neal as the Lakers won 65 games in the regular season, and then dropped the Orlando Magic 4–1 in the NBA Finals.

# GLOSSARY

**assist**
A pass that leads directly to a basket.

**blocked shot**
A play in which a shooter's field-goal attempt is knocked down by a defender before it can reach the rim.

**defense**
The act of trying to stop your opponent from scoring a basket.

**dynasty**
A team that wins multiple championships over a short period of time.

**rebound**
A missed shot that is caught by a player.

**rookie**
A first-year player in the NBA.

**steal**
A statistic awarded to a player who takes the ball away from an opponent or intercepts a pass intended for an opponent.

**veteran**
A player with a lot of experience.

# FOR MORE INFORMATION

## Further Readings

Birle, Pete. *Boston Celtics (On the Hardwood: NBA Team Books).* Minneapolis, MN: MVP Books, 2013.

Silverman, Drew. *Basketball.* Minneapolis, MN: Abdo Publishing Co., 2012.

Silverman, Drew. *The NBA Finals.* Minneapolis, MN: Abdo Publishing Co., 2013.

## Websites

To learn more about NBA's Best Ever, visit **booklinks.abdopublishing.com**. These links are routinely monitored and updated to provide the most current information available.

# INDEX

## ABOUT THE AUTHOR

Will Graves grew up in a family of basketball players and spent his childhood hoping his Washington Wizards would win the NBA title. He has covered sports since 1996 and joined The Associated Press in 2005. He spent six years covering basketball in hoops-mad Kentucky and now works in Pittsburgh, where he tries to teach his two children the value of the bounce pass.